Leaving Our Shadows Behind Us unveils, as time and space become fluid and malleable, the rustling of uncensored leaves of a poetic album that conjures up haunting scents, sounds, tastes, colors, and sensations of the poet's past and present, from his childhood home in Asingan, Philippines, with undeniable Ilocano roots, to the hardships and abuses of the OFW (Overseas Filipino Worker) in the Middle East, and to daily scenes of life in Hawaiʻi. Unexpectedly, images of violence against animals and man burst before your eyes. At times, traumatic memories reveal scars that possibly have yet to heal. And yet, the reader will encounter humor through odes dedicated to bedbugs, termites, rats, fish, and unforgettable Filipino characters that the author has created and put forth on the compelling pages of this collection.

—Edwin Lozada
President, Philippine American Writers and Artists

Elmer Omar Bascos Pizo's first book celebrates an intimate regimen through rituals and ethnic peculiarities valued as his personal touchstones for being Filipino. The senses urge him back to memory's homeland through poems that stir the belly's hunger, summon a recollection of landscapes left behind, or make us wince because of the hand's costly errors, as well as the cold-shouldered dismissals of the greater world. Yet these are not soft-lit poems of an alluring misty filter. The poet trades in roughness and impurities, too. Here, tone reconciles the contradictions of humor, anger, sarcasm, self-irony, and wit born out of pride and clumsiness. Pizo tackles the dismissive world for belittling all that it finds strange.

—Danilo Francisco M. Reyes
Ateneo de Manila University, School of Humanities

"The art of losing isn't hard to master," Elizabeth Bishop wrote, though she hardly meant it. The shadows that Pizo tries to leave behind in this autobiographical collection are those of country, an angry father, violence against persons and animals, guilt, racism, self-hatred. "I owned the wound, / I owned the stitches, / I owned the discomfort. / Worse, I owed him the money." What better way to express the pain of exile and colonialism? But even in "Stitches," Pizo surprises us with his wit, having asked for Levi's stitches, not the Wrangler's he got. Pizo's poems are plain-spoken, but hardly plain. The poems are blunt, but the poet tender. A wonderful addition to Bamboo Ridge's chorus.

—Susan M. Schultz
Tinfish Press

Elmer Omar Bascos Pizo's "Identity" posits to be one "wiggling in the beak of a maya bird, / ... the desperate earthworm / struggling to be free." It's an apt metaphor for the Philippines beset by corruption, poverty, hunger, and a "common people / pining for a *genuine* people-serving government." Yet the beauty of these poems makes them like "the gardenias, ylang-ylang, waling-waling, / sampaguitas, and camellias [with] coveted nectars." With their unforgettable imagery that can elicit empathy from a wide variety of readers, these powerful poems become like bagoong "smelling like a mouse / rotting in a pool of brackish water" and yet that remains a "favorite dipping sauce." Dip into these poems for an important read. I've been aware of Pizo's poetry for years, and *Leaving Our Shadows Behind Us* is a long-overdue début: "where blood / drains in its purest state."

—Eileen R. Tabios
Author of *The In(ter)vention of the Hay(na)ku*

This collection of biographic poetry is a confluence between art and science, a fusion of raw scientific observation to that which is creative and artistic. The death of formalism is imminent at the turn of each page giving way to new flavors of artistry that deviate from the rule of verse. A precarious sarcasm springs forth from the persona's rich sojourn as a native Ilocano OFW whose reminiscent experiences served as catalyst to turn in a work that laments ethnocentrism, concomitant hardships, and injustices while mocking mediocrity at the peak of its arrogance. Wounded/inspired in its tone that emanates from a rough childhood, countless struggles working under the scorching heat of the Middle East towards the freezing cold and laborious journey in the West, this artwork is a sacred protest against structuralist thinking—conjuring up a fight against long-established dogmas that never question the definition of uprightness in religion, culture, and the socio-political, while bridging the gap between that which is scientific and humanistic in nature.

—Maria Christina A. Calachan
Educator/Department of Education/Region I
Urdaneta City, Pangasinan, Philippines

LEAVING
OUR SHADOWS
BEHIND US

Elmer Omar Bascos Pizo

Bamboo Ridge Press

ISBN 978-1-943756-00-1

This is issue #114 of *Bamboo Ridge, Journal of Hawaiʻi Literature and Arts*
(ISSN # 0733-0308).

Published by Bamboo Ridge Press
Printed in the United States of America
Bamboo Ridge Press is a member of the Community of Literary Magazines and
Presses (CLMP).

Typesetting and design: Misty-Lynn Sanico
Cover art and design: Napunako Sanico
Cover photo and weaving pattern courtesy of Wikimedia Commons

The script ꦠꦤ that appears in the section breaks of this book spells "Pinoy" in
Baybayin, an ancient pre-colonial Philippine writing system.

Bamboo Ridge Press is a nonprofit, tax-exempt corporation formed in 1978 to
foster the appreciation, understanding, and creation of literary, visual, or
performing arts by, for, or about Hawaiʻi's people. This publication was made
possible with support from the Hawaiʻi State Foundation on Culture and the Arts
(SFCA), through appropriations from the Legislature of the State of Hawaiʻi
(and grants from the National Endowment for the Arts). Additional support for
Bamboo Ridge Press projects and events provided by the Hawaiʻi Community
Foundation's Baciu Cultural Fund and Robert Emens Black Fund and the
Hawaiʻi Council for the Humanities.

HAWAIʻI
STATE FOUNDATION on
CULTURE and the ARTS

HAWAIʻI COMMUNITY
FOUNDATION

HAWAIʻI
COUNCIL
FOR THE
HUMANITIES

Bamboo Ridge is published twice a year.

For subscription information and back issues contact:

Bamboo Ridge Press
P.O. Box 61781
Honolulu, Hawaiʻi
96839-1781

808.6261481
brinfo@bambooridge.com
www.bambooridge.com

5 4 3 2 1   19 20 21 22 23

ཕྱིན

FOREWORD

The poems in Elmer Omar Bascos Pizo's first collection, *Leaving Our Shadows Behind Us*, cannot be characterized as lyrical or beautiful, for they are painfully honest and bold, even harsh. On one level, some of the poems can be considered sardonic, on another, humorous. Whatever the reader's perception may be, the conclusive opinion about these poems is that they are different, often provocative or sad in their rendering.

Pizo's poems are divided into three sections. "Black Dog," the first section, contains poems about his identity as a Brown Filipino man in the Philippines and America. "The Whipping Rope," the second section, addresses the physical abuse he and his mother encountered and endured under the harsh hand of his father. This theme of violence and abuse is then extended into a larger context— that of abuse thrust upon immigrant workers—in poems that recount Pizo's experiences, as well as those of other immigrant workers who were incarcerated and tortured in the Middle East. The third and last section, much lighter in tone, is appropriately called "All of God's Creatures," and contains poems about animals and people, mainly in Hawai'i and the Philippines. Through his poems, Pizo celebrates an ongoing legacy of hard-working Filipino immigrants and their growing communities across America, and in a broader sense, the world.

As Pizo wrote these poems, he had to work through the issues of writing in a second language about his and other immigrant workers' experiences. Writing his work in English has been a feat in itself, for Pizo had to reprocess what he understood in Ilocano and Tagalog and reinterpret his understanding into idiomatic English for himself, as well for that of the English reader. He worked diligently to keep his interpretations as authentic as possible. He tried to keep the nuances found in his dialect, often concerned that readers of English may not understand the hidden meanings found in the Filipino language, much like the kaona found in the Hawaiian language. To aid readers, the meanings of Ilocano, Tagalog, and Arabic words are included immediately following some of the poems.

Additionally, in many of his poems, Pizo plays with stereotypes of the Filipino male. He is self-deprecating and funny in many of these instances. It is as if he is taking ownership of the stereotypes to lessen their power and their effect, especially because of those who wish to use them to condemn or make fun of members in the Filipino community. Along with the stereotypes, he talks about the injustice and prejudice Filipinos often encounter as migrant or immigrant workers. Perhaps he uses stereotypes, especially of the Filipino male, to show us how complicated and challenging dealing with stereotypes is.

Pizo's book is an important book for everyone, especially for those in the Filipino community here and those working in various parts of the world. His work gives us a glimpse of the hardships many men and women face when they leave the Philippines and go out into the world. We cannot stress enough the need for books like Pizo's, which document and perpetuate the Filipino community's culture, traditions, and heritage of hard-working people.

Juliet S. Kono
Christy Passion
Editors

CONTENTS

Black Dog

The Whipping Rope

All of God's Creatures

Black Dog

Sibulan

Negros Oriental, Philippines

At the mouth of the sea
where the Ocoy River ends,
brown bodies of naked boys
pop in and out of the swirling
water, like fish gasping for air.

Foaming soapsuds stained
with dirt from clothing
women scrub on the river banks
dissolve in the green water,
like this half spoonful of sugar
I just dropped
into my cup of tea.

Identity

From the venerated stones of my river
where mudfish bump hibernating catfish,
where spiders in muddy rice fields weave their geometric webs,
to the volcanic fires of Mayon, Taal, and Pinatubo,
the verdant forests of the Cordilleras,
the variegated blues of the Pacific Ocean and South China Sea,
surrounding the islands of the Philippines,
this is what I am:

The Atang that wards off evil;
the Gulgol that helps in grief when one's head
is washed in the river with burnt rice straw;
the Bari-bari that drives out spirits
that may harm newcomers to the place.

The Lagdaw-kilawin: fresh-water shrimps
marinated in calamansi juice, sukang iloko,
siling labuyo, and chopped onions.
The Dinardaraan: pig's stomach, small intestines,
meat, liver, cooked in vinegar, sea salt, and blood.
The Pinakbet—a mix of skinny eggplants,
tomatoes, and bitter gourd cooked with bagoong.

The common folk who still gargle water scooped
with coconut ladles from clay water jars,
instead of the Nescafé vintage drinking glasses of the 1970s.

The dried hands of mothers mending
tattered clothes beside flickering kerosene lamps
where gullible moths are tempted to flirt
with deceitful flames.

The shrill laughter and sing-song rhymes
of skinny children whose distended bellies
and protruding eyes conceal the strangling power
of hunger, parasites, and pain.

The preying mantises in dignified-looking
suits and barong tagalogs, holding office in posh
buildings, pretending to be lawmakers
while they pad their bank accounts
with money stolen from government coffers,
private businesses, and the poor people
of my exploited Philippines.

The overworked carabaos and cows
beaten again and again by farmers
who have buried their conscience
deep into muddy fields.

The secrets, the whispers of the common people
pining for a genuine people-serving government,
as in the aspiration of stray dogs for a fresh bone;
roosters, hens, and chicks, scratching
the face of Mother Earth for food morsels.

The gardenias, ylang-ylang, waling-waling,
sampaguitas, and camellias whose coveted nectars
are taken by greedy bees and butterflies,
just like what our megalomaniac leaders do:
bleed dry the defenseless, the poor.

Wiggling in the beak of a maya bird,
I am the desperate earthworm
struggling to be free.

Atang – An offering of food to honor the memories of dead relatives
and/or to ward off evil spirits. The most common types of food offered
are sticky-rice balls, hardboiled chicken eggs, and chicken wings and
drumsticks.

Gulgol – A ritual to ward off bad luck. Specifics vary with province or region. The day after the funeral, relatives of the deceased wash their heads in the river or the sea using burnt rice straws to remove bad luck.

Siling-labuyo – A condiment made from wild chili peppers, minced garlic, and vinegar.

Sukang iloko – A dark yellow vinegar made from fermented sugar cane juice used for pickling.

Barong tagalog – Filipinos don this formal wear for private and state functions. This clothing is woven from pineapple leaf fiber or banana silk.

Ylang-ylang – The fragrant night-blooming flower of the cananga tree.

Waling-waling – An orchid belonging to the Vanda genus. It is considered "Queen of the Philippine flowers."

Sampaguita – Also known as Arabian jasmine. It is the national flower of the Philippines.

Maya – A catchall term for a variety of small common birds, such as sparrows and finches.

Brown

I.
Why is the Manong's skin not white,
like the color of milk?
Brown, brown, nothing else!
The color of his favorite barking pet,
the color of Hawaiian Host Chocolate Macadamia
his nieces crave for in the Philippines.

Brown. The color of a Manang's dried-up tears
after dancing into the early hours of morning
at a Korean bar on Keʻeaumoku Street.

Brown. The color of dilated pupils
in a Manong's eyes.
He uses bato day and night.

Brown. The color of his favorite dipping sauce
his wife calls bagoong, smelling like a mouse
rotting in a pool of brackish water.

Brown. But flushed, the color of the Manong's face
as he insists he is innocent
when the manager of Island Recycling
has found a discrepancy in the weight of five rubbish
bags of crushed soda cans the Manong just sold.
The manager carves out the crumpled bottom
of one can then another,
corn-sized pebbles falling out of them.

II.
   Psssttt, pssssttt! It's not the pop-up tab
of a soda can. It's a Manong calling out to his friend
seated on a bench, waiting
for the The Bus on Alakea Street.

Psssttt, psssttt, pssssssttt! Hooooooyyyyy!
They're the same sounds the Manong hears,
as he walks the cobbled path of Fort Street Mall,
forcing him to stop and check
where the *pssst-pssst* had come from.
    Oh, it's Madame Aurora. He had met her once
at Costco Salt Lake where he helped her
load 55 bags of Hinode rice into her Honda Civic.
At the time, rumors of an impending strike
by Honolulu Longshoremen were floating around.
    Why you gib me a wrong numberr? she complains.
    I was trrying to kol you to phyn
    ip yo want to buy my eksas bags op rice.

III.
Rice or without rice, bagoong or without bagoong
the Manong is not a bit concerned. He will survive.
He can run underground drug stores,
peddling *da kine*, you know,
what the man-in-blue calls *ice.*
Or he can grow weeds with five-fingered leaves
hidden under dense foliage of bitter melon vines.

Thin and elastic, like the stretched tongues
of lizards snapping unwary flies,
girls and boys,
clinging to urine-damaged lamp posts on Hotel Street,
roll dried buds the Manong supplies
into joints they smoke like ordinary cigarettes.
The smoke clears their clogged sinuses,
and they swear,
brings them closer to heaven.

IV.
The Manong, losing a sizable amount
betting on an illegal Sunday cockfight in 'Ewa Beach,
later finds himself in Pearl City seated at a karaoke bar,

18

taking swigs of gin and tonic spiked
by sips of Heineken to fire up his subdued spirit.

   Ahem, ahem, he coughs.
Suddenly, he stands up
and sticks his flat ʻōkole way out.
He closes his eyes, watery from thick smoke.
He opens his mouth
and begins to sing "My Way".

   My pren, ay sey it kler, ay stet my kase
   op wits aym sertin.
He lifts his closed right fist,
suggesting an invisible microphone.

Ear-tickling accents and bad enunciation
disregarded, wild applause and catcalls
from the tipsy audience
drown out his wailing voice.

He nods, he smiles. He stomps his extra-wide
feet, waves his callused hands, enjoying
the misplaced adulation, forgetting for a while
he's still a brown Manong, as he belches out
the last line of his song: *ay did iiit myyy weeeyyyyyyy!*

   Tenk you beri mats!

Manong – An honorific used to address an older brother in the
immediate family or an older male relative from the extended family.

Manang – An honorific used to address an older sister in the immediate
family or an older female relative from the extended family.

Stones of My River
November 2007

Hey, that brown guy just came from P.I. His beard and untrimmed moustache speak volumes. Ice! It must be hidden somewhere. Sniff his face, check under the roof of his tongue, inside his nose or ears. Ha, ha, ha, ha! Look at him, he looks like a goat. Must have chewed a lot of weeds in P.I. Get closer. Sniff his butt! I can hear him, what the U.S. Customs guy at the baggage claim section of the Honolulu International Airport is saying in loud whispers to his K-9.

Don't move, the Customs guy barks. Standing straight, I spread my arms. Shit! I scream to myself, as the dog sinks his fangs into the cheek of my left butt. *Why? Is it because I'm brown? What makes it unlawful to be a brown man?*

Where is your bato? Not waiting for my answer, he stabs the side of my box with a cutter. He rips the flaps. Dried pusit, chicharrones, bibingka, tupig, old family photographs, my shirts, pants, and soiled socks and briefs spill from its gut. I remain standing, staring at his nose.

Where's the bato? the Customs officer asks again.

Inside that small backpack, I say, pointing to it with coned lips. Using his cutter, he splits it open. Five pebbles I took from the Chico River fall and scatter. *These are the batos I'm carrying with me!*

Those stones had been my only tangible link to my revered river, the river where I learned to hold my breath underwater; the river where I panned gold dust from mine tailings in the hinterlands; where, on clear nights, from its rocky banks, I counted the stars until my eyes became crossed; the river where I brought Fernando, my water buffalo that pulled the plow all day; where some of my childhood friends took for granted its calmness and lost their lives. Good swimmers, they did not heed its width and depth.

The K-9 sniffs one pebble after another. It sneezes. The Customs guy, not finding anything illegal on me, turns his back, followed closely by his K-9 and two associates, handcuffs and 9mm Glocks dangling from their waists. I stare at their disappearing backs with pent-up anger. It seems only Filipinos are harassed, often treated with contempt and disdain.

As I collect my scattered things, a petite Asian woman offers her plastic grocery bag. *Thank you*, I say and smile. All my things in hand, I drop by the washroom to offer a small prayer:

O Lord of the black, gray, brown, olive-green, red, yellow, white skin.

O Creator of fleas and ticks and blood-suckers, I've always treated people of different color with respect, but like many Filipinos, how I hate my brown skin.

Don't get me wrong, but I can't hold off any longer from asking You: *is it a sin if I pare down this brown skin from the top of head down to my toes and change it into some other skin color to stop others from taunting and disrespecting me?*

Bato – Term for rock or stone.

Dried pusit – Fresh caught squid, which are cleaned, salted, and then sun-dried.

Chicharrones – Pork rinds—pig skin, sometimes with meat, boiled in salt, dried under the sun for a day, and deep-fried.

Bibingka – A rice cake made from rice flour, water, sugar, cheese, and grated young coconut. It is baked in a container lined with banana leaves.

Tupig – A rice cake from Pangasinan province made of glutinous rice flour, water, coconut milk, sugar, and young coconut, wrapped in banana leaves and cooked over a charcoal fire.

Lauyang Manok

After I pluck the feathers off—
an inch below
the chicken's ear where I slit—
I place a bowl
of fragrant diket,
with a light sprinkle of asin,
where blood
drains in its purest state.

When the Lauyang Manok
is cooked halfway
on the fire stove, I scoop
the coagulated blood
and place it in the pot
to simmer with green papayas,
bok choy, chili leaves, banana peppers,
and patis.

When cooked,
I put a small portion of the blood,
together with the chicken's boiled liver,
wing, head, and heart on a saucer,
and place it beside an unopened
bottle of Ginebra San Miguel.

Chanting *Umay kayon Apo*,
I call out the anitos and other spirits
to come, partake of the food,
drink the gin,
and ask them for protection
from lurking demonyos.

Diket – Aromatic, glutinous rice.

Asin – Sea salt.

Lauyang Manok – Chicken soup seasoned with sautéed ground pepper, garlic, onions, fish sauce, ginger, chicken liver, and salt.

Ginebra San Miguel – A brand of gin manufactured in the Philippines.

Patis – Fish sauce used in cooking, especially sour broth dishes like fish sinigang.

Umay kayon Apo – A chant calling spirits to partake in a meal.

Anitos – Invisible wandering spirits.

Demonyos – Evil spirits that inflict harm.

The Plow

I was twelve, Father,
when you brought me to the rice fields
for a lesson—
how to push a plow.

Watch them, you ordered,
referring to the farmers,
their webbed feet sinking with elegance
in the wet, soft earth like mud-coated
ballet dancers behind plows
dragged by loyal water buffaloes
that left rows of upturned soil,
neat as a six-year-old girl's braided hair.

When I gripped the plow's wooden arm,
and tugged the rope
looped around the buffalo's nose,
I took three or four steps before
the plow nose-dived into the soil,
and the blade broke in half
with a sharp *krrraaakkk!*

I threw you a furtive glance,
afraid you could already be
a raging pit bull,
raring to plant its teeth into me.
Instead you hollered:
    Son, how do you expect to eat rice
    when you don't know
    how to prepare the soil?
    You should be ashamed of yourself.

Scarecrows

We scarecrows, propped up alone or lumped in groups of twos or threes
in the middle of the rice fields,

feel all right even though we can't exchange glances, talk to each other,
or walk away from the fields.

We are spared from the need to drink water and eat rice and kaldereta.
We are spared from jealousy or needing a wallet full of cash.

We are spared from laughing at a friend's laziness then crying with him
when he loses his job. We are detached from any binding feeling of love

or to be loved, to get married, and have families for the rest of our existence.
Every day, we wear with pride our knitted beanies

woven from every color of yarn imaginable or hats woven from straw,
and our long- or short-sleeved shirts,

oversized gowns and trousers with disgusting tears and holes.
Some of us sit on stilt-like chairs, some stand on one leg,

others hold hands as if they are lovers, fearing the other would soon slip
away from their grip. A slightly bent figure, can be seen in the distance

propped by a pair of wooden crutches. Looks as though something
must be wrong with his knees.

That tall guy in the center of the field holds an empty bottle of San Miguel Beer.
He looks dehydrated from staying so long under the sun.

Day in and day out, we're out there, in the fields, without any protection
or shield from the prevailing heat or cold.

Sometimes, the rain falls and soaks us from head to straw feet and the wind
doesn't care either. It just blows until our flesh of hay

is scattered about, leaving our straw-stuffed bodies badly disfigured.
We don't give a damn if our shadows are the only things that are real.

We don't have names, identification cards, faces, skin, bones, hands, feet, genders or ethnicities.

Nothing provides us a deeper sense of purpose other than to scare the birds away.

Kaldereta – A goat stew with potatoes, carrots, pineapple chunks, red and green bell peppers, tomato paste, tomato ketchup, and salt.

Toothless

From the image taken
the dental assistant possessing
the keen eyes of a fighting cock
notes one of my bicuspids
is leaning—with scary resemblance
to a termite-infested utility pole—
toward the second molar.
The receding gums,
the weakened roots,
are almost beyond control,
caused by years of neglect,
creating plaque
from pieces of impacted food.

Sworn enemy of tooth decay,
Dr. David Breese
remains unrecognized
as a tireless savior
of defenseless teeth.
Armed with a square mirror,
stainless-steel pick and hook,
top-of-the-line x-ray machine,
precision drill, and cutting edge
skills and techniques,
including a squad of dental
assistants speaking in foreign
tongues, he is ready,
not only to arrest the leaning,
but also to crown this tooth
without the elaborate ceremony
fit for a Middle Eastern King—
to retrieve it from further ruin
and save me
from a toothless grin.

Altar Server

St. Vincent Ferrer
Old Town, Dasol Pangasinan

The tiny bronze bells
in my hands—
for a few minutes,
remain silent.
Father Rudolph Alvano,
is about to end swinging
the censer back and forth.
The bells' ringing,
a strictly observed Anglican
and Catholic tradition,
...must accompany the smoke of the incense,
with prayers of the Saints
in their ascent before God.*

While kneeling, I fall asleep.
  Thwack!
The often genial, septuagenarian priest,
officiating the Holy Mass,
delivers a resounding slap
on the back of my head.
He hastens to the pulpit.
With livid eyes he strikes out:
  My dear brothers and sisters,
he says, his voice crackling like fire,
  I found it very disconcerting
  to see a fly on the back
  on Elmer's head
  and couldn't wait
  for the good Lord to do something
  to remove it.
  To me, a fly is a nauseating
  manifestation of the devil.

As you have heard and seen,
I took matters into my own hands.

Oh, my Lord, I murmur,
let me say something.
This is a sham,
a perfect charade.
Father Rudolph Alvano,
may be a man of God,
but he lies through
his false upper teeth!

*Revelation 8:4

Circumcision: Pagtutuli/Pukpok Style

What about Juan, the tuli drop-out, who opted for anesthesia,
sterilized surgical scissors and pharmaceutical ointments? An
outsider to the barkada (clique) who shared the same ritual, he
is called "O.R." with reference to the Operating Room and the
attending nurses. In June, the young men will enter the freshman
high school class. Some will strut, knowing that the others know.
What an achievement!

—Penelope V. Flores, PhD,
Professor of Education Emeritus
San Franciso State University
Excerpt from *Filipinas Magazine*, May 1995
"Circumcision: Writhe of Passage"

Summer 1989

I.
In a secluded spot
near the Chico River,
a group of pukpok-circumcised boys,
direct vigorous, high-pitched
sing-song chants,
   Supot, supot, supot!
   Kamatis, kamatis, kamatis!
   Duwag, duwag, duwag!
urging boys age 7 to 15
to fall in line,
be circumcised,
for nothing is more shameful
than a boy whose tuli's not done
in the pukpok style.

   Pwuehh!
The rust-colored bitter juice
of a betel nut the manunuli had been chewing
for more than an hour, lands on the dirt,

31

as he instructs the first boy:
Look at the sky.
Stay calm.
In a minute this will be over.

The small pamukpok in his hand
strikes at intervals—Pok! Pok! Pok!—
the back of the newly-honed razor blade.
Three inches of cut foreskin
hangs from the boy's organ.

What good does it do
to a boy, aged fifteen,
if the upper portion
of the stretched foreskin,
covering the tip of his boyhood,
looking like a sick bird,
resting on the lukaw driven
into the ground by the manunuli,
is cut with an unsterilized labaha
without help of an anesthetic?

   Aray! Aray ko!
Blood gushes from the wound.
The boy goes limp,
loses consciousness.

II.
This pukpok style,
grants him the irrevocable license,
to show off that mutilated thing
between his legs
as an authentic badge
of pride and courage.

A month later, you will hear him
bragging to his friends:
You want to see?
The thing's handsome
without its helmet on.

Tuli – Term referring to the action of being circumcised and the act of circumcision.

Supot – Uncircumcised.

Duwag – Coward.

Kamatis – Tomato.

Pukpok style – Circumcision performed with a mallet and a razor blade.

Pagtutuli – Term referring to the act of circumcision.

Lukaw - An L-shaped wooden stake made from the guava tree.

Manunuli – The man who performs this traditional act of circumcision.

Labaha – Razor blade.

Pamukpok – A small wooden mallet.

Aray ko! – An exclamation. Loosely translates to "Ouch!"

Stitches

Splitting wood for firewood
with a twenty-five-pound broad axe
one humid Sunday afternoon,
I almost severed my right foot.
It was probably the bad swing
I took or because of the tough
fibers of the knotted milo wood.
My bluish vein, spurting blood,
was no different
than the pulsating artery of a hen's neck
cut open with a skinning knife.

Not daring to make a comment
about my forthcoming stitches,
I scrawled on a sheet of paper
my request:
   Doctor, please, Levi's style.
   More durable, more dignified,
   more beautiful.
He nodded but had something else in mind.
Proceeded with the sewing of my foot
by pulling the lacerated flesh together
and stitching up my wound,
Wrangler style.

What else could I say?
He owned the needle,
he owned the anesthetic,
he owned the catgut,
he owned the antibiotic.

I owned the wound,
I owned the stitches,
I owned the discomfort.
Worse, I owed him the money.

Mother Tongue

So many F-words.
So many S-words.
So many words loaded with worms!
Sick and tired of hearing
them spill out of his mouth,
Mother, instead of dialing
a call center for help with disturbed kids,
took the initiative to correct
my 4-year-old brother's behavior
before too late.

She made an urgent *Come to me*
gesture. *Stick out your tongue!*
she commanded, her left hand
tightening its grip on the sides
of my brother's lower jaw.
    Arayyy! The instant pain
left his angelic face distorted,
him crying.

After rubbing, like sandpaper,
a handful of sea salt over his extended
tongue, *Here, gurgle your mouth with this*,
she demanded, handing him
a bottle of cane vinegar soaked
in siling-labuyo, red-devil pepper.

    Uhu, uhu, uhu, uhu, uhuuuuu!
The concoction burned the inside
of his mouth, as mucus dripped
out of his nose. He spat the liquid out,
hitting her face.

Her eyes burning,
she pinched his ears,
and pulled them apart like a rubber band.
All the while she was screaming:
  You're not my son!
  Tang ina ka. Tang ina ka.
  Tang ina mooooo!
  Your mother's a whore!

First Day of March, 1987

That Sunday morning, right in the middle
of our animated conversation—
matched with an occasional slapping
of each other's hands, wagging of our index
fingers, and the shaking of our heads—
you suddenly grabbed your buttocks,
then screamed, your eyes rolling up,
baring their whites.
I took you into my arms, but didn't know
where to place your body.

Barely audible, the chirps of birds.
Less, the buzz of mosquitoes, the wing-hum
of dragonflies.
No late crows of roosters, no *krraasssh-krraasssh*
of mango leaves brushing against
the corrugated metal roof overtaken by rust.

You were unable to say anything,
the Halls Mentho-Lyptus lozenge still melting
on your stiffened tongue,
your half-consumed Marlboro cigarette
on the concrete floor, releasing smoke
that sashayed to the ceiling.

My younger brother wasn't home,
delivering roses and calla lilies
in another town.
Mother was in the kitchen,
frying eggs, with four-year-old Ruth
snoring in her sleep.

Black Dog

Yes, I'm a typical dog eater,
often considered
the most shameful remnant
of the human race.
There's no need to defend myself.
It's useless.
But, once and for all,
I want to set
things straight
about this black-dog thing.

I don't know how
or where this notion—
that Pinoy dog eaters in Hawai'i
prefer a black dog's meat—
came to be.
It could have been said in jest,
by a loose-mouth Pinoy:
  It makes us stronger,
  more virile, especially in bed.

In the Philippines,
a dog's color doesn't matter.
Some are raised as guards or pets,
some, for eating,
like cows, pigs, and chickens.
A dog's tender, fragrant meat—
a delicacy that melts in the mouth
when roasted, then cooked,
asocena or adobo.

So what's the big deal?
May the dog be tame or wild,
trained or neglected,
smart or stupid,

purebred or mutt,
yellow, black, brown, or spotted,
when you roast its skin
it always turns black.

Asocena – A traditional style of cooking in which a dog's meat is cubed and then sautéed with garlic and onion. Water, soy sauce, and black pepper are then added. It is brought to a gentle boil until the sauce has cooked off.

Adobo – A traditional style of cooking in which a choice of meat is cut into pieces and sautéed with garlic, peppercorn, soy sauce, vinegar, salt, and bay leaf.

The Black Dog and Wallace Stevens' Blackbird
From a Brown Man's Perspective

1.
It's not my intent, Sir,
to discredit you or your poem.

Please pardon me if I insist,
but I really don't see your blackbird's eye,
as *the only moving thing among*
twenty snowy mountains.

2.
Is it possible your attention
is so fixated on the blackbird
that you fail to acknowledge
the presence of a black dog,
shivering under my thick fur coat?

3.
His tail isn't wagging.
His black eyes are the only ones
moving like the *eye of the blackbird.*

4.
You may find it difficult to believe.
Way back in Hawai'i, the black dog and I
had made up our minds
that once we set foot in Connecticut
we'd case some fowls
trapped in *barbaric* snow.

5.
Sir, my black dog isn't listening
to *the blackbird whistling.*
He doesn't have to.
He's just waiting for the blackbird
to hop off your poem's *cedar-limbs.*

6.
Whether it's a pellet gun
or a .22 caliber rifle,
the black dog knows I'm a poor shooter;
much more now,
since visibility is near zero.

7.
What I don't get,
like you, the black dog is of *three minds.*
What makes it more difficult to understand,
he's not even involved in what you know.

8.
The black dog's eyes aren't moving,
glued to that black thing disappearing
in the thickening snow.

9.
Still shivering,
he rubs his eyes with both paws.
Really, it's not easy to accept
your blackbird having already left.
But its *small part of the pantomime*
isn't over yet.

10.
I guess, without your blackbird,
he doesn't know what to do.
His mind is only whirling
and whirling and whirling.
in the freezing snow.

11.
Sir, like your blackbird and
that *man*
and that *woman,*

the black dog and I, a brown man, also
are one.

12.
If things don't go right
and the black dog and I are trapped
here in the cold for a number of days
with nothing more to eat,
although a difficult decision to make,
Sir, I do want you to know
the black dog is very aware
of what I'm going to eat!

*Italicized words are from Wallace Stevens' poem, "Thirteen Ways of Looking at a Blackbird."

ហៀបហ

The Whipping Rope

My father's belt,

a Hickok
three-inch-wide
brown cowhide,
made in the USA,
could hold up pants
with a forty-two-inch
waistline.

No one was bold enough
to challenge the throne of my father,
ruler of unspeakable tyranny,
adept at squeezing
every ounce of fear from us
in his imaginary kingdom.

The smallest
mistake could cost
his subject of ire
twenty-five to fifty whacks.
I have collected
these difficult-to-heal
scars in my psyche.

My father has been dead
more than thirty years;
yet, in my flesh,
the welts and bruises
remain purple, blue,
red, and black.

Haunting Manifestations of Your Temper
On Father's 26th-year death anniversary

I.

Hold on tight to your club.
Keep an eye on that rat!
Born and raised here in the rice fields,
it's perfect for the palate!
Your booming baritone barked orders,
shoving into my young brain
a lesson on survival.

The rat sprinted away,
faster than Usain Bolt in the 100-meter dash.
Before I could apologize—
Whack! Your club landed
on my left shoulder blade.

II.

Your familiar booming voice woke me up:
The ones you chopped, earlier,
are not enough to heat water
for tomorrow morning's bath!
Under your watchful eyes,
the *tsak-tsak-tsak* of wood being split
with my ax,
broke the silence of the night.
I was twelve years old.

III.

During the Angelus,
I was the church's designated bell-ringer.
Half deaf, I made sure none of the beats
were skipped, the tempo kept,
because, with a minor mistake, you would scream,
bang the wooden walls of the belfry
for me to get it right. After the final ring,

my steps on the double, I ran down
the winding stairs to kiss your hand
and Mother's. Failure to do so
was unforgivable. And I was late.

Reciting *Our Fathers* and *Hail Marys*
didn't help the cause.
My hands cold sticky,
I proceeded straight to the bench
beside the dining table. Pulling
down my shorts to my knees,
(to show no cardboard was sandwiched
between my flesh and shorts)
I bent over and lay on my chest.

While your leather belt
walloped my butt,
I thought about a time
when I waded in the Chico River
and chanced upon a pair of kanduli,
playing hide-and-seek
behind moss-coated stones.
Thinking of the fish
numbed my pain.

Leaving Our Shadows Behind Us

After yet another whipping, I got up, pulled up my pants, and said the obligatory *Thank you*, giving Father my word: *I will not forget to give my respects to you again.* I then kissed the back of his hand.

As if on cue, Mother appeared from behind the curtain. Leaving our shadows behind us, she led me toward her kitchen sanctuary. Not a single word or whisper came out of her lips; all I could hear were a succession of labored breaths. I lay on a bench, as her right hand grasped the neck of a beer bottle and swung its bottom against the flame of the lamp to melt the solidified extract of coconut oil.

Between sobs that shook my shoulders and tears clouding my vision, I took a fleeting glance at her. Ridges and folds of wrinkles, raw cuts and scars marred her beautiful face. Struggling to pour the oil into the palm of her left hand ruined by a web of broken lines, she whispered: *Everything will be all right. Everything will be all right.* I gave a slight nod. It was the only thing I could do, careful not to expose the disbelief bottled up in me.

Looking at the bluish-purplish bruises on her arms and shoulder, the fresh, inverted L-shaped cut below her left eyebrow, the swelling on her upper lip, what I saw was more hurting than all the pain Father inflicted on me.

Father, Was I Not Your Son?

There was a night, when you,
showing no signs of anger,
suddenly exploded,
leaving me buried in tons of sulfuric words.
   Son of a bitch!
   I don't want to see your face!
   Get out before I smash your skull
   with a dum-dum bullet!
Your cheeks and the bulging arteries
in your neck, purple-red.

How could I silence your rage?
Was I not your son?

A fully loaded .38 Special S&W revolver,
was now your favored weapon
to torture me.
To show off in front of your drunk buddies,
you yelled, *kneel!*
Then pressed the gun's cold muzzle,
hard, against the back of my head.

   Click!
Not knowing
your gun wasn't loaded,
for all I knew,
I was already dead.

The Revelation

After science class with Madame Corazon, my godmother and teacher in Grade VI, she asked me if it was true that my mother had run into a low-lying mango branch: *Are you both doing fine at home?*

With her hand covering the side of her mouth, she spoke to me in a whisper:

Did you know, your mother, made helpless by your father's almost-daily beatings, once left him for Villasis, her parents' home? She took you with her when you were only one-year-four-months old.

By year's end, your father went to Villasis to get her. He went down on his knees and begged her to come back to him, swearing on a crucifix he wouldn't lay a hand on her again. Moved and convinced by his gesture, your mother, Comadre Betty, packed up your things, took you into her arms, and went back to Asingan. Your grandparents pleaded she not go back with him. Three weeks later, and for no reason, the punching, slapping, and hair-pulling began again.

Your father didn't recognize you as his. Perhaps he saw other men in your face: her former boyfriend, the janitor in our school, or the town's coffee bean vendor.

Forgiven

Although rows of flowering roses, orchids, native hibiscus
in black five-gallon plastic pots lined the back and sides
of the yard, it remains a mystery to me, Father, as to why
the gardenia was your favorite flower. Day old, dried, or fresh,
you strung and hung them in your bedroom windows to soak
in their scent, often mistaken for the soft smell of death.

The snub-nosed barrel of your .38 Smith & Wesson revolver
on the reading table served another purpose.
You stuck gardenias in the open barrel
like a vase lying on its side. Isn't it ironic,
considering it was the same gun you pointed at our heads—
mother's, brother's, and mine—at the peak of your unprovoked
rages.

If you weren't talking about your gardenias, you talked
about bullets that exploded upon hitting the flesh,
which gave glow to your ashen face, as you proudly showed them
to your freeloading drinking buddies over cold bottles of San
Miguel Beer.

And when you died, I picked the last of the flowering gardenias
to line the inside of your custom-made, bare-wood coffin.
Although I gave preference to an opened gardenia
to adorn the right pocket of your pin-striped suit, I pinned
a purple phalaenopsis tied with a black, silk ribbon over mine
to let people know I was in mourning.

Father, even if the cruelty you left behind remains an uncut
umbilical cord connecting you to our memories, this phalaenopsis
on my chest signified not only my grief. It also meant
I had forgiven you before hatred could fully take over my heart.

Yellow Carpenter Bee I

Right after
the long struggle
to free yourself
from the fangs
of certain death
in a trap set
by a camel spider,
you shake your wings,
testing to see
if they retain
strength enough
to rise up
    and fly off
in the smoldering
morning wind.

Naked Pictures
Mawasim, Riyadh 1985

Upon getting up from kneeling
to kiss the desert sand
after arriving in Mawasim
for the first time, I find myself
surrounded by bearded strangers
with concerned faces.

I greet everyone: *Sabah al-khair, sadik.*
There's no response.
I only hear the whirling desert wind,
and noise from the fingers of a plump,
stunted Thai, scratching
his dandruff-crusted head.

A lean, haggard Pakistani asks,
his bloodshot eyes glued onto mine:
    Do you have naked pictures from P.I.?

His tongue licks the whole
width of his upper lip
like that of a car's wiper blades.
    Sadik, he adds,
    I prefer ones with the sixty-nine act.

When I see eyes like that,
all I want to do is clamp
the person's head with both hands,
like a vise grip,
and ram it straight into the wall,
but what can I expect
when someone had been stuck
in the desert two or three years
without seeing
members of the opposite sex?

Not uttering a single word,
my hands rip off the white lining
of my scarlet jacket. Glossy pictures
of Pinoy porn actors
and Pinay porn actresses
in compromising postures—
        the sixty-nines,
        the helicopters,
        the parachutes—
fall out like leaves.
Name them, I have them.

Suppressed lust has broken loose!
To grab one of the pictures,
        fingernails dig faces,
        fists smack heads,
        feet slam chests.

Sabah al-khair – Good morning.

Sadik – Friend.

Mafi Mushkila

Hayathem, Saudi Arabia

I.

How many times have I told you,
I scold myself—*you're not a kid anymore.*
Why waste your tears over not getting paid again?

II.

Yalla! Yalla!
Antoine, the Lebanese foreman,
yells at me to hurry,
interrupting my self-rebuke.
Katir siokol! He admonishes,
pointing to the pile of camels' waste.

III.

Mafi yalla, yalla! Sui, sui, Sadik!
No need to hurry, I shout back
and wave my hand in defiance.
Muk mafi! Mafi pulos, mafi siokol!
Idiot! No money, no work!

IV.

You—Muk mafi!
His dagger eyes stab mine,
as he punches the air.
You a whore! he cusses.
Mafi mushkila! I yell back,
kicking the sand in disgust.

Mafi – This is a combination of *ma* and *fi*. Ma means "no/not/none." Fi means "there is."

Mushkila – Problem.

Mafi mushkila – Literally, "there is no problem." However, it may be used as sarcasm to mean the opposite.

Yalla – Come on, let's get going, and/or hurry.

Katir – So much, plenty, and/or big.

Siokol – Work.

Sui – Slowly.

Sadik – Friend.

Fulus – Money.

Muk mafi – Non-standard phrasing. No brain ("muk" means "brain"), stupid, idiot.

Horses in the Shape of Clouds
Hayathem, Saudi Arabia

An hour before closing time.
In the motor pool, waiting
for my turn to fill the metal belly
of the John Deere tractor,
I take a quick
sweeping look at the sky.

Strange!
Horses, in the shape of clouds,
galloping towards the East.
They must be heading back
to their homeland after reality
kicked in about this sterile place:
   Grass doesn't grow in the Asir region.
I drop my head.
Weeping, I remember *home.*

Yesterday, the messenger
from the Arabian Agriculture's office
in Mawasim delivered letters from P.I.
Mother's letter was scalding:
   More than nine months since you left,
   and you haven't sent any money yet.
   Have you forgotten us?
   You're such a thankless wretch,
   a plain son-of-a-bitch!
   Your father suffered a stroke.
   He slurs his speech; he can't lift
   or move his left leg,
   and is paralyzed.
   The hospital bills are staggering,
   his medications costly,
   my savings account, empty.

I look again at the sky.
Defeated by thirst
and hunger in a futile attempt
to find their way back home,
the horses are moving in circles.
My tears keep falling.

Al hamdu Lillah! Sadik, hina fi moya?
Please, I'm so thirsty.
A Yemeni laborer—
an inch taller than the four-foot handle
of the shovel he's carrying—
interrupts my mourning
for Father.
Myself.

Al hamdu Lillah – All praise be to God.

Sadik – Friend.

Hina fi moya? – Do you have water with you?

Moya – Water.

Triple Itch

Here in the Kingdom,
where even a photo of a female's exposed legs
is seen as evil and the root
cause of corruption,
a guy who indulges in porn,
and is caught,
would be whipped by the mutawa
fifty or more lashes every Friday
while jailed 3 to 6 months
by the Sharia court.

It's an open secret among Pinoys.
Bootlegged videos of Filipino couples—
writhing, wailing, wrestling,
in unembarrassed bliss—
are available to anyone drooling to see them.
For free!

Here we are,
more than a hundred deprived men,
the only females we have seen
the last two years
were camels, sheep, and goats
we fed daily with bales of hay
imported from European countries.

Despite fighting off the aches
of having toiled under a scorching sun,

despite the danger
of not being sure who
the in-house spy is among us,
every Friday,
after dinner in the cramped mess hall,

we take the enormous risk
of watching these XXX-rated videos.

To help us find relief after the movies,
the camp manager, Engineer Pedro,
holds three impromptu contests.
   One: *Who would be the first to ejaculate.*
   Two: *Who could squirt their semen farthest.*
   Three: *Who could eject the most semen after he exploded.*

Bets are placed.
From Pedro's own pocket, the monetary prizes
for the 1st, 2nd, and 3rd place winners:
riyals, dollars, dinars,
even the weak peso from the Philippines.

Mutawa – The Islamic religious police who enforce adherence to Sharia
law.

Riyals – The currency unit of Saudi Arabia.

Dinars – The currency unit of several countries (formerly of the
Ottoman Empire): Algeria, Iraq, Jordan, Kuwait, Libya, Macedonia,
Serbia, and Tunisia.

The Beheading

After the 9:00 a.m. Salah

Over six feet tall,
thin as a reed,
your black, deep-set
eyes stared lifelessly
at the people
anxious to watch
your execution.

Blindfolded and kneeling,
your body slouches
over your knees,
almost touching
the concrete floor
of the *chop-chop*
square.

The gaunt cop,
with his croaking voice,
reads from a paper
printed in Arabic script:
    You killed a man.
    You are now to pay
    for it with your head!

His hands holding tight
a long, curving sword,
the swordsman
positions his feet,
making sure his
stance is correct,
before he lifts the sword up high
to swing the blade down
in one swift stroke
to the base
of your neck.

Thug! Your head,
severed cleanly
from the neckline,
falls and rolls to your
right. Blood gushes.
Your body
and lips twitch
then go
still.

The Arabs clap, dance,
and hoot.
Others shout:
  Allahu 'Akbar!
A few Pinoys
throw up.

My stomach churns,
my knees turn
into gel.

I fall with you.

Salah – The times when Muslims perform their five daily, obligatory prayers.

Chop-chop square – A wide, open space in Riyadh where beheadings are often held.

Allahu 'Akbar! – God is [the] greatest!

Ghost

Arabian Agriculture Company
Mawasim, Riyadh

An hour more, and this twelve-hour misery
disguised as work, is again over,
backpack sprayers, leaf cutters,
shovels, and hand-tillers
cleaned and stored.
Filipino, Thai, and workers
from across the Middle East
pile out of the greenhouses,
carrying the weight of blisters,
insect bites, and ugly dog-bark-calls
from the Arab Masters.

In silence, we walk in twos or threes,
going back to our segregated dormitories.
We follow three kilometers of darkness
on a trail of twirling sand made worse
by the stifling evening heat.

Some of us go straight to the bathrooms,
others, their bedrooms to read letters.

Like me, some need to satisfy their hunger.
We head for the mess hall like beggars
and eat whatever is served—
bloody chicken stew, the normal fare.

Done with my food,
I get up from the dining table,
bring my tray to the dish-washer's rack,
say thanks to the cook finishing his smoke,
and head back to my dormitory
to take a quick bath to wash off
the dust and grime before going to bed
with the mosquitoes.

The letter to the Saudi Ministry of Labor
I started writing three weeks earlier,
is not done yet, the list of complaints
having increased five-fold.

With no crowd jostling for space,
no out-of-tune singing,
no grunting or grating sounds,
the bathroom is mine.
I can linger and waste
all the water I want.

I turn the faucet on,
cup my hands to wash off
the layered crust of brown dust
on my face.

When I check my face in the portrait-size
mirror mounted above the sink
facing the front door,
a lean six-foot figure
with deep-set eyes,
wearing a gray kandora,
stares at me.
A tangled salt-and-pepper beard
and sideburns enhance
the looks of his mournful face.

I look toward the open door.
No one is there.
I turn again to the mirror.
He is still staring at me.
He moves his hands,
as if he wants to grab my neck.

Kandora – Traditional Arab male's robe.

Abdul Wahid ibn Abdul Rakman

Rakman was not easy to accept as a master
of the fabled double-talk,
because he sounded so sincere.

At his place in the desert for the first time,
we lined up in front of his office
while his puppets collected our iqamas,
work permits. He forced us to sign
another set of contracts
in Arabic script with no English translation.
  If you don't sign your names,
  I'll send you back home after you serve
  time in the much-dreaded hotel of Arabia,
  the kalabooz,
he growled.

He listed our Employment Agreement:
  Free plane ticket to the Kingdom,
  meals, lodging, and medical service,
  unlimited overtime,
  paychecks handed out on the 30th,
  45-day paid vacation and free plane tickets
  to one's country of origin
  and return to the kingdom.

  Allah forbid,
  if something should happen—
  a free coffin and the shipping
  of the body back to the Philippines.
  If you sign now,
  in a month's time,
  you'll begin harvesting green bucks
  without working.
  That's your sign-up bonus.

Abdul Rakman wagged his index finger
to make a point.

I signed my name.
Rakman grinned.
Since that time,
we'd been toiling 10 hours a day
for 6 days in sweltering heat.
For 9 months,
not even a dollar had been handed us.
Worse, Rakman reduced our pay.

Six people packed our 9 × 11 rooms.
We ate scrambled eggs for breakfast, chicken stew
for lunch, chicken adobo for dinner with half-cooked rice
garnished at times with creamy
maggots sporting horns;
also, served fish of unknown origin
smelling of ammonia. Prior to freezing,
they must have been rotten to their bones.

The sign-up bonus, paid vacation, weekly living allowance
and free plane tickets to a worker's
country of origin and back?
   Pfffft! Cancelled without notice.
It was probably true for the free coffin
and shipping of one's body to the Philippines.

These Arabs,
sipping tea in the comfort
of their water-cooled offices, had assumed
it was their sole right to shove and slap us around,
do whatever they wanted.

For a hundred halalas
our masters bribed a few fellow contract workers
who did a good job
manufacturing accusations against us.

These masters thought we contract workers
were lambs or goats bound at their feet
to be slashed across their jugulars,
as offerings,
making sure the desert bloomed.

Kalabooz – Jail or prison cell.

Allah – God.

Halala – A currency unit of Saudi Arabia. 100 halalas is equal to 1 riyal.

Whipping Rope

The whipping rope,
forty-eight inches in length,
is slender
and tapers at the end.
But, *uh-uh*, don't ever
underestimate its strength.
When it strikes its target area,
all the nerves there
lose their throbbing
innocence.

For almost a year,
while we were on
ten-hours, six-day work
weeks in glass greenhouses—
we were still waiting for our pay,
still eating rotten fish
and rice sprinkled with sand.

My conscience often spoke to me,
Forget about working.
Stand up to the bosses
Instead of sulking and grumbling,
STRIKE!

If the watermelons, cucumbers
tomatoes, cantaloupes die,
so be it.
If you are imprisoned,
so be it.

Every Friday at 9 a.m.,
after the Salah, the time for prayers,
we, prisoners,
were herded like smelly goats

from our holding cells
to the main square,
to take our individual punishments
for crimes,
real or perceived,
they had accused us of committing.

Mine was real.

Fed up with the farm's working conditions,
I led a work strike.
No one tended the crops.
It was less than a week before
all the fruits and vegetables
withered.

Ten successive lashes
crisscrossed my bare back.

Each time the whipping rope landed,
sometimes striking the bone
of one of my shoulder blades,
my body shuddered.
I clenched and tightened my fists.
How I wanted to cry and scream!
But I knew the Lord was watching.
It was disgraceful for Him
to see me acting like a child.

With my hands
tied to a black-painted
$4 \times 4 \times 6$ post,
I struggled to stand upright.

My tormentor pulled my head up,
looked into my eyes with the sharpness
of a Henckels knife.

He taunted:
Oh, my boy.
How I love your nerves and flesh.
They're so tender and supple.
I'm working hard on them
to make your suffering more unbearable.
Be still.
Fifteen more and this will be over.

Midpoint

Al Kharj, 1985

Thamaniya arba'aoon, forty-eight.
Two more strikes, *khamsoon,*
and the whipping reached its end.

Today had been the mid-point
of sixteen Friday whippings.
Today, the rope looked so much longer.
Today, the rope felt so much thicker,
and I was only halfway through!

As soon as it landed,
the rope, sneaking up from behind,
was like the stretched tongue
of a Komodo dragon
licking my back.

Clenching my teeth,
all I could see were the eyes of my father
as he stared into nothing,
and my mother's in her disappointment of me.

The whipping finally over,
my hands were numbed
by the tight ropes.
The Yemeni guard untied me
from the six-foot post.

My body crumpled.
Sadik, moya, please,
I moaned, then coughed,
clearing from my throat
a clump of coagulated blood.

Before the bearded mutawa
could stamp his size-twelve footprint
on my back,
the Sudanese laborer,
still shaking from the lashings
he also received,
rushed forward to help me on my feet.
Taal sadik, he said,
extending his scalloped hands.

After a couple of labored steps,
I stopped to catch my breath.

Khamsoon – Fifty.

Moya – Dialect. Water.

Taal – Come.

Yellow Carpenter Bee II

You,
in erratic flight
through the scorching wind,
spot a cluster
of flowering milkweed
just below
the closest sand ridge;
your anxiety builds.
The ancient gods
and goddesses
have listened
to your prayers.

Relax, they say,
all the nectar is yours
for the sipping.

Remembering Sanabel

As I remember Sanabel, it went down like this: we first met one early morning when the driver and I, employed by a farm in Riyadh, were unloading crates of tomatoes, cantaloupes, and cucumbers at your family's grocery store. We also helped to stock the empty produce shelves.

You boldly asked me, *What's the hole in your face?* I looked around me; I was puzzled. You may not have fully understood my concern. More than three hundred lashes and months of jail time if I got caught talking to you wasn't worth it, no matter how beautiful you were.

By that time, you had removed your niqab. I got back to you with a nervous smile for I wasn't certain as to what you were asking me about. *What's the hole in your face?* you asked once more. This time, your index finger pointed at my left cheek.

Oh, it's not a hole. It's a dimple, I said, unsure if you understood me. Sanabel, the magnetic pull of *fooling* myself in love was so powerful, I couldn't resist it. Though I knew it was wrong, I was sucked into it. But I also knew I should not do anything about these feelings. Therefore, before my next thrice-a-week turn to deliver crates of fresh harvests to your store came around, I talked to Nasheem, my senior Pakistani agriculturist, to send me to Al Kharj instead, to look at the progress of our nursery project there.

When I came back to the farm the following week, the driver handed me your letter. It was in a pink nameless, address-less envelope with three red little hearts in the upper right-hand corner. It came with a little bag of grapes, figs, dates, and oranges. *I wish you to get well soon*, the note said. *I hope it was nothing serious.* The farm's driver apparently said I had been sick when you inquired why I was not helping with your deliveries. You made it clear in your last paragraph that you wanted me to come and see you before you left for London in two weeks.

Though I had sealed my lips about our attraction to each other, I had to admit, Sanabel, I was afraid for us. We would not have been able to stop and things could have gotten very dangerous.

Niqab – A veil worn by a Muslim woman in public that covers her face, with the exception of her eyes.

All of God's Creatures

Pinay Preacher Across Aʻala Park

At the intersection of North King and South Beretania Streets,
in front of a row of convenience stores
and small restaurants near a bus stop
under the metal awning of the Tong Fat Company,
a twenty-something Filipina, barely five feet tall,
including the three-inch clogs she wore,
caused a stir among the day-shift workers
waiting for The Bus to take them to their workplaces,
mainly, the posh hotels lining Waikīkī.

As she preached, her alert eyes
rolled from side to side,
watching people carry brown paper bags,
as they walked out of Lyn's fast-food restaurant.
She probably assumed they had ordered
pinapaitan, pork guisantes, and dinuguan.

    You know what? she screamed,
her tightly clenched fist slamming the top
of a makeshift lectern:
    Aside from loading your arteries
    with wicked levels of cholesterol, the Bible says
    blood and innards of beasts are filthy.
    Consuming them is highly offensive
    to the Holy Spirit. Whoever is guilty of this,
    they will be swept up and collected like ants
    and thrown into a pit where
    there is uninterrupted roasting
    and grilling of gluttonous souls!

But no one was listening to her;
something else had caught their attention.
Their eyes were held on the slit to the right
of her yellow hibiscus-printed,
black ankle-length skirt.

At the top of her inner thigh,
a mothlike patch of black hair,
popped in and out,
whenever she moved.

You should have seen the eyes
of the portly mainland tourist
standing beside me.
He was leaning on the creosote-smeared utility pole,
and wearing an aquamarine shirt that read:
    IF IT SWELLS, RIDE IT!
He may have not been aware of it, but his eyes
were dangling half out of their sockets,
an obvious sign, demons
were growing wild inside of him.

He was not alone.
I almost had to gouge
my own eyes with a fork
just to move them away from her thigh.
Matthew 18:9 was firm on this:
    If your eye causes you to sin, tear it out
    and throw it away.

Instead, I forced my eyes to follow her
right index finger held above her chest,
as she rocked it back and forth like a metronome.
Rocking her finger this way
showed the onlookers her self-righteous
interpretation of the verses she had randomly
lifted from the pages of her King James Bible
marked with notes.

It was a warning:
    If you didn't flee from your lust and desires,
    the devil was itching to bring you to hell.

Pinapaitan – A bitter soup made from the organ meats of a cow, goat, or rabbit. The primary source of the bitterness is the bile or the cud extracted from the animal's stomach.

Pork Guisantes – A dish in which strips of pork are simmered with green peas, bell peppers, tomato sauce, salt, garlic, and onion.

Dinuguan – A dish of sliced pork and organ meats cooked with pig's blood, vinegar, salt, and green chilies.

Death of a Cardinal

His elegant red mitre, the color of fresh blood,
flashes like fire, as he leaps and bounces
between the soft branches of the puakenikeni.
He's not looking for worms,
he's looking for a mate.
just listen to his call—a short squeaky note—
as if something's stirring deep inside of him.
Every now and then,
he turns his head to the left,
then right, then left again.

A brown-skinned boy who looks
like a recent immigrant,
places a select stone from a pouch
onto the soft leather pocket of his slingshot,
takes a deep breath and holds it
while he pulls the twin yellow rubber bands to their limit.
Only a slight quiver of his right hand
gives away his excitement.

  Hey! Stop it! I jump up.
Scream to distract the boy.
  Shoooooo!

Tiny feathers float, drift,
then settle on the ground.
A few land on the blades of grass,
some, on the head and back
of the grazing goat.

I hasten to the spot
where the cardinal's body has fallen.
Though limp, the bird is still warm,
blood gushing from his left eye.
The bird has a deep depression
on the left side of his head.

I cup my hands around his body
and deliver a succession of long,
controlled blasts of air onto his face.
After a time, I stop to check for signs of life—
a slight twitch of the legs,
movement of the eyelids.
I beg for a miracle and mercy.

I want to hold the boy
accountable for the cardinal's small death,
but he runs away—
is it from the devil or to him?

Kailua Goat

Forty kilograms in weight, the goat is laid on a makeshift wooden
table, its mouth gently shut. Without hesitation, my cousin punctures
its carotid artery, draining its blood. The blood is saved. I want to turn
away, but I don't. I follow the torching of the hair, the scrubbing and
separating of the skin, the removing of the legs, horns, head and
innards, and the cleaning of all the parts before they are made into
dishes over bamboo fire pits and slow burning coals. The men gather
over the fire. They honor the goat this way.

> —Madeline Farin, author of *The Philippines: the*
> *Food and Farmland of Santa Catalina* (5/18/2016)

Before the caretaker caught him
by his horns
and dragged him bleating
to the makeshift table,
he was jumping,
running back and forth,
kicking up dust with the other goats.

One hundred seventy-five bucks,
including tax, maybe with some hidden fee involved,
that's all it cost me for the right to do *anything*
I wanted with his ten-month-old body.

With his fore and hind legs bound
together by a nylon rope,
his body is forced to curl like a fetus
inside a mother's womb.

Just as my friend is about to push
the pointed tip of the stubby ice pick
to punch a hole into his jugular,
I place my left hand over
the right side of his chest
heaving with fear.

Not to assure him everything would
turn all right, but to let him know
I do sympathize with his inevitable fate.

Flame from a hissing blowtorch
melts thick strands of black hair
around the neck, belly,
chest area, sides of the ears
hooves, and whole length of tail,
giving off a sulfuric smell,
suffocating me and my friend
doing this horrid thing to him.

The shrinking jaws,
misaligned teeth,
heavily stained green by months
of chewing grass and weeds
appear as the sole bearer of truth:
  The goat seems to be smiling,
  enjoying the burning.

Chicharrones

I.

Since the day you were born
I assumed, without question,
the role of caregiver,
kitchen help, nurse's aide,
never failing in my duties
of disposing in appropriate manner
your discouraging messes;
handling your vitamins,
antibiotics, and supplements;
cooking your daily staple
of rice porridge, boiled eggplants,
raw sweet potatoes,
and finely chopped swamp cabbage;
providing you with warm baths
after coaxing you out of solitary
confinement, that tiny pen
of bare metal and concrete.

II.

To keep your cholesterol level in check
you had to stretch your joints and muscles daily,
do some vigorous pushing and digging
of dirt by means of your snout.
I stayed close to your side,
monitoring your blood pressure
and temperature, how fast your
heart beat, how fast your breath
rose and fell.

III.

In five years, you turned
from a twenty-five-pound weakling,
into a more than 330-pound marvel
of lard, bones, and meat,

and you mated, without reservation,
with promiscuous boars,
and like a machine
gave birth to multiple litters.

My advancing age and the rising cost
of feed, medications, booster shots,
and other miscellaneous operating
expenses got me worried.
No one would believe the cost
of raising just one baboy.

IV.
So, if by chance or intent,
someone set his eyes on you
and initiated haggling with me
as to how much you would cost
based on your live weight,
and should the price be right...
   I'm so sorry, so sorry!

V.
In spite of your vehement
objections and boisterous cries,
there was nothing I could do
after I got paid.
The lucky buyer,
anxious to make a quick profit,
swiftly secured your legs
with a nylon cord before he lifted
you up by the ears.
His assistant grabbed
you by the tail in attempt
to distribute your weight,
while the buyer struggled
to load your wobbly body
into the back of a beat-up

Isuzu pickup truck.
I rode in the back with you
to the slaughterhouse
a couple of miles away
where waiting butchers' gowns,
splattered with blood and flesh,
hung on huge thick hooks.

VI.
I watched as the men
worked under the prying
eyes of flies that managed
to squeeze into the room
shielded by inadequate screens
meant to be protective.
The butchers guided
their power saws and cutters
with hands that exuded
the confidence of years
of experience and in efficient manner,
sliced up your warm carcass
into choice pieces.

Pork butt, belly, shoulders,
chops, bones, loin, sirloin, tenderloin,
ribs, eye of round, ears,
tail, snout, and other parts of
your face ended up in sanitized
styrofoam plates, the sticker
price for each pound and
the bluish seal of the FDA
stamped on them
and shelved in open-case chillers
at competing supermarkets.

VII.

Not to be outdone, a Filipino guy—
grateful to maintain
sanitation and cleanliness
in the slaughterhouse
for the minimum wage
of five dollars and twenty-five cents,
having come, barely a year ago,
from a country
where nothing goes to waste—
melted down your fat under
the intense heat of a China-made burner,
fat that had grown solid in your gut
through years of worry-free existence.
The man collected your melted fat
into an iron vat and into this oil,
he fried and crisped strips of your skin.
Later, he offered me the crunchy bits.
I could not bear to eat them.

Undressing Chickens

To undress chickens,
the water they are dipped in
must not be too hot. Otherwise,
it makes it difficult
to pluck their feathers.
Make sure the fine feathers under the wing pits
around the neck, butt, and breast
are also removed.

If you can't, then pass the chicken
over a flame to singe it.
This may burn the skin,
but don't be concerned. The burnt
hair and skin will enhance the smell
and taste when it's finally cooked.

Here's an important thing to learn:
make an incision on both sides
of the opening where a hen lays eggs.
Then, pull out everything inside its belly
all at once. Watch out for flies!

Mother, I have stored these reminders
since I was a seven-year-old kid,
helping you prepare food for guests or relatives
who dropped in at ungodly hours
from distant provinces, unannounced.
You had to interrupt my sound sleep
so I could go out and catch a hen
or pullet from their kagab,
their bamboo cages.
I can't imagine how many
chickens' lives were sacrificed.
I protested, remember?

I even let one fly away into the darkness,
as I was about to chop its neck.
But you dismissed my protests,
saying: *That's just the way it is!*

I now undress leghorns and culls
for a locally owned, wholesale-retail
poultry company in Kalihi.

What can't I come to terms with?
I no longer feel squeamish about killing chickens,
except for when I pull out a chicken's intestines,
and see the livers, crops, gizzards, yolks,
slither out. And those damn flies—
they are like the freeloaders who came to our home
or like buzzards on overhead electrical wires—
that waited to land and lay
their eggs on parts
I had already sorted and cleaned.

Balut

Balut is a developing duck embryo that is boiled and eaten out of its shell. Some Filipinos consider it a delicacy and an aphrodisiac.

I. Candling
The way my coarse hands—
wrinkled and scarred
by years of hard labor
digging graves,
pushing plows,
pounding steel
for arches and fences—
are held up and move so delicately
with skill and precision
the dome-shaped end
of the duck's slightly mottled
egg close to the twitching light
of the red candle
is a marvel to me.
I give all of my effort
to detect any vital signs of life,
like feathers, beaks, and feet,
in the orange glow of yolk
after it had been sat on by its mother
for eighteen days.
But once in a while, I must freeze my breath,
because I'm reluctant to say: *Tsk! No good!*
And as if it were a softball,
toss out the bad egg
into the garbage can,
its embryo,
looking more like a grown chick.

II. Eating Balut
To the uninitiated, I suggest
a fourteen-day-old duck egg.

The feathers aren't long.
The beak, eyes, wings,
legs, feet, and claws
aren't prominent. Yet.

Tap the round part of the shell
against any hard object—
a table's surface,
the side of a beer bottle,
a spoon, the handle of a knife.
If there's nothing you can use,
your forehead will do.

Once cracked,
peel the shell off
until a hole appears.
Tear the semi-transparent
membrane, add a pinch of salt
and slurp the brown juice
of the egg until nothing's left.

Peel off more of the shell
until the yolk
attached to the embryo is exposed.
Ignore the black threadlike
veins wrapping the yolk
and the surrounding
rubbery albumen.

If I were you, I'd close my eyes,
suck the whole embryo
and creamy yolk all at once.
Doing this, you'll be spared from
looking at a half-eaten embryo,

Hereafter, there's nothing much you can do.
Your stomach will probably feel queasy
and you may regurgitate

the contents in your belly,
the gastric juices going up
past your jerking esophagus,
the balut finding its way
out of your mouth
and if unlucky, your nose.

But once you've eaten it,
there's something compelling about its taste
that in time
would make you want to try it again.
And again.

Pan de Sal: Bread of Salt

Manny's Bakeshop and Restaurant

September 18, 2015
     9:00 a.m.
Acknowledged master of sweets and breads,
of measuring cups and flour sifters,
Manny Pakyao, Head Baker,
had yet to report to work
after he took an unscheduled
leave, seven days to date.

In spite of the five to ten
daily messages left on his cell phone
by Rhodora, the worried owner,
an answer from him
had yet to materialize.
Business was brisk.
Rhodora had no other choice,
but to ask the baker's helper,
Omar Filipos, with only
3 months of on-the-job-training,
to step up,
become the Head Baker,
though unsure how he would do.

     10:00 p.m.
He was still working at this hour.
After sprinkling a pinch
of coarse salt over the last
of the thousand lumps
of cupcake-sized dough
for the Pan de Sal,
Omar Filipos, wiping his sweat
and humming the same tune since he began
kneading at one that afternoon,
finally called it quits.

He could now have his six bottles
of Heineken and grab some sleep
that had eluded him
the past couple of nights.

September 19, 2015
       4:00 a.m.
Omar Filipos's head was twisted
to the left of the kneading table,
and from his open mouth, saliva
dripped, like watery glue from a tube
without its cap on.

Under the table, like gangs
of thieves, red and black ants,
fought each other
over old, stale crumbs
strewn about the sandaled,
callused feet of Omar Filipos.

A lone buzzing mosquito
took a bite of Omar Filipos's receding
forehead. Suddenly opening his eyes
he slapped the area where
he first felt the mosquito's itchy sting.

Meanwhile, the refrigerated batch
of salted lumps of dough
taken out to sit on the baking table
in the warm air—taking a cue
from the stored power of active yeast—
rose high above the petty squabble of ants
and the errant mosquito.

Bedbugs

don't just stay in beds
all day, all night.

Have lots of traveling
to do, by bus, boat,

and other ways.
Even person to person.

From Hilo to Kahului,
Līhuʻe to Waikīkī,

Los Angeles to Atlanta,
and around the world.

Reykjavik not on that list.
The place too cold.

Dar es Salaam, Cairo,
Rabat, Kinshasa too hot.

Rome's not included.
Bedbugs don't seem to care

about creating trouble
for the Pope.

If they happen to cling
to his most blessed robe,

it's certain he may pray
hard for them to be

vanquished from the dark
and into the light of day.

And if weather permits,
they could hitchhike

to the International
Space Station and sip

vodka-tainted blood
from the Russians.

Then to the moon—
to understand the pull

of gravity so they can be
better at sucking more blood

from their innocent victims.
They seem to travel

without regret, shame,
or reservation,

and hitchhike because
they're born that way,

hiding in suitcases,
clothing, pillow cases,

under the soles of shoes.
But they especially like garments

waiting to be washed and kept for days
in overflowing laundry baskets,

where they hide, sleep,
and of course, procreate.

Termites and Filipinos

If a Filipino is a buk-buk, what do you call Filipino children?
—Frank de Lima

I.
A piece of wood,
hard or soft,
pressure-treated or certified—
you can't leave it on the ground.
Hiding under misleading branches of mud tubes,
subterranean termites move
in stealthy ways.

A termite,
though it doesn't know
how long, tough or thick
a piece of wood is,
will always yield
to its unmatched destructive ways.

Going through their daily crawl,
termites don't slow down
except to hug and smell each other
or stop to embrace
and gossip with other termites.

Avoid being lured into thinking
your home is going to be fine.
You're dealing with termites, right?

Watch out!
In spring and fall,
winged termites appear
in the company of their lovers,
brothers, sisters,
relatives, and friends.

Keep an eye
on the opening and closing
of a termite's mouth.
That mouth,
only a few microns wider
than a dot, is brutish in its charge
on a piece of wood.

If you do nothing to deter them,
they will claim
a sizeable portion, if not all,
of respectable pieces of wood
that hold the structural integrity
of your house.

II.
Termites and Filipinos
can never be friends
unless they iron out
the folds and kinks
found in their differences.

Rest remains a four-letter word
devoid of much meaning
to a hard-working Filipino,
even less to a termite.

Toothless and blind,
gobbling wood day and night
is the termite's main business,
assuring their colony's storage chamber
swells to the brim.

And the Filipinos?
When the sun barely opens
its cantilevered eyelids;
or when the moon

hides itself behind darkness,
they're still given to the task
of wiping butts, cleaning toilets,
washing dishes, clipping grasses,
folding linens, or making up soiled beds,
content only to line their pockets
with thick wads of hard-earned cash
to send to their extended families
desperate for help in the Philippines.

Buk-buk – Dry wood termite.

Rodent Control
Pier 2, Honolulu Harbor

Just before noon,
I lifted the lid of the black bait station
I set three days ago
under an abandoned stairway
in the back of the aging two-story building,
bordering the right side
of Aloha Tower Marketplace,
identified by the foot-sized,
Calibri-type lettering:
Department of Transportation - Harbors Division.

Inside the box,
I found the corpse of a rat,
stiff in its fetal position,
as if it were shielding itself
from an imminent,
but unknown threat.

Tilting my head
to grab a better look,
a small smudge of coagulated blood
is barely visible at the base
of clumped whiskers
on the left side of its face.

There was no hint
of even the slightest pain, except that
its exceptionally sharp front teeth
were protruding—
as if resting after having gnawed death—
solid, hard, indestructible.

Its nose was blunt, fur brownish,
tail flaking, balding, and shorter

when measured against its body
that was a little larger than a mouse's.
And two small, round, shiny objects
below the base of its tail disclosed
what it was. A juvenile male
of the Norway species.

I assumed his parents did not fail
to repeat warnings to be wary,
not go into strange
boxes sitting harmlessly
along the edges and corners
of commercial and private establishments,
but of course, they went unheeded.

In this mix, a solitary housefly
hovered low then high,
or when circling, tight then wide
above the corpse.
The smell of decaying flesh,
likely picked up and carried by the wind,
beckoned the fly inside the neglected backdoor.

I barely opened the mouth
of an improvised body bag
when the fly began barreling down
several times before executing an imperfect
loop a few feet away from the corpse
already in rigor mortis.

The fly darted away
in response to my presence
then flew back toward the rat.
It hovered directly over
the corpse for some time before it moved
into a straight nosedive
to quickly plant what looked like a light kiss,

as if saying farewell,
on the corpse's furry forehead.

There was no way for me to understand
the fly's intent or for me to know
how to respond to its understanding of life.

So, when it directed its eyes up at me,
I bowed, then looked right back at it.

Catfish

A tapered pole from an aged
Chinese bamboo stalk
he cut not long ago
from a clump growing
wild in upper Nuʻuanu
leans on the far end
of the porch, its leftover bait
of a horned beetle larva
being nibbled to its creamy
core by hardworking red ants
and a family of shameless flies.

Catfish, with eye sockets
an eighth of an inch deep,
cut lengthwise
with a good German fillet knife,
are hanging like bats on a wall
of woven black bamboo slats.

Sitting still,
waiting for its chance,
a Siamese cat,
yawning
once in a while.

Tilapia

Novaliches, Metro Manila

At the corner of the sidewalk
where I am standing,
a woman is selling tilapia
from two galvanized tubs
marred by nail-size holes.
A thin layer of crushed ice
spread over the dead fish
helps maintain their freshness.

The light from a lone candle
jutting out from the neck
of a 7-Up bottle
penetrates the dwindling ice,
refracts through the slime
overlaying the tilapias' dark-gray scales,
glides through the gloom
looming over their faces,
then settles in their eyes
that seem to be gawking at flies.

The fish grab the attention
of a handful of passersby
off from work in nearby factories.
They stop. They ask:
  Where they come from?
  They still fresh?

Showing sincere interest,
some of them squat,
and with their pointer fingers
poke the flesh, part the cheeks,
and inspect the gills for redness.

Her left hand swatting flies,
her right cradling an infant,

106

the vendor, in her early twenties,
struggles to make up her mind.
Even at forty pesos a kilo,
whatever profit she projects
in earnings will quickly disappear.
If she doesn't give in,
most of her fish would remain in the tub
until the morning.
A chest freezer or upright refrigerator
is real
only in her imagination.

Adding greater pressure,
the shorter of the scissor-shaped
hands of the clock hanging above
the fabric store's entrance across the way,
is already moving away from seven.

Firefly

Sunday Evening, Asingan

By the half-opened
capiz-shelled window,
a pretty,
twenty-year-old
morena is right
in the middle
of taking off her yellow,
sweat-soaked blouse.

Her blue skirt,
lying
crumpled at the foot
of her waiting bed.

Shy, fearing
she may think of him
as a pervert
if she saw him
peeping through
the half-opened window,
the lone firefly
promptly turns off
his flickering light.

Capiz – The translucent shell of windowpane oyster, which is used as a
glass substitute.

90 Degrees Fahrenheit

'Ewa Beach, Hawai'i

A thick powder of dust at 'Ewa Mahiko Park,
obscures fragments of feathers
floating above a dry bed
of Bermuda grass where a pair
of common sparrows
are rolling over and over,
like small empty barrels
blown about by unharnessed winds.
Getting up, the birds,
through stroking dust
off their feathers,
extend their legs and take turns
scratching each other's backs.

This scene brought me
back to a neighbor
in Asingan, Philippines:
a bedridden,
seventy-year-old man
and his thirty-something wife
who took him for better or worse.
He was a retired dishwasher
from the Rainbow Lanai,
at the Hilton Hawaiian Village in Waikīkī.
Working five days a week
for thirty-three years on his feet
and doing yard work Saturdays and Sundays,
he got up with the sun
and ended his work day with its setting.
He went back to the Philippines
to live the good life with his new wife.

Outside the couple's living room,
in a narrow patio fronting their lawn,

a self-taught guitar player of limited fame,
chasing a Civil Engineering degree
at a university nine miles away,
offered to teach the young wife,
without pay,
how to play classical guitar.

During breaks from her lessons,
she could be seen with her head
held up high and eyes closed,
as he lightly scratched her back,
like the sparrows in 'Ewa.

Once in a while,
within earshot of her poor husband,
her smiles turned to loud giggling.

Asingan – A second-class municipality in Eastern Pangasinan,
Philippines.

Viagra

I.
What good does it do
for a man sixty years of age—
widower for the last ten,
retired from his full-time job
and walking with a cane—
(rheumatoid arthritis
hadn't stopped stamping
its authority over his left knee)
to get back to P.I. to marry
a woman forty years his junior,
defying, in the process of bringing her to Hawai'i,
all kinds of pointed questions and hassles
from the U.S. Naturalization and Immigration Office,
wanting proof the marriage wasn't fixed
for convenience, and that their union
was consummated before he brought her
back to Hawai'i after a three-and-a-half-year wait?

Right after his good friend set him up
with that woman back home,
it was difficult to understand why this
being taken advantage kind of stuff,
more than anything else about her,
was not the man's main concern.
For heaven's sake!
He should have known better,
especially when stories
of these kind of marriages usually didn't end well.
    And they lived happily ever after
was often out of the question.
More likely, the usual ending was:
    See you in court!

a divorce occurring three years after a woman's
permanent residence status was changed and once
she had secured her much coveted prize:
that of U.S. citizenship.

II.
Aside from having reached the age
of not knowing how to handle
the romantic side of love anymore,
like giving small packages of sweet
nothings with light kisses on
the forehead and cheeks,
one of the main tools of his trade,
once formidable and up to par
in meeting any challenge,
had not recently passed any window
of opportunity for its use.
It was sad to say
it had been reduced to a jack
that could no longer lift!

He did everything to
ensure she not leave him.
In preparation,
he indulged in bowls of shark fin soup,
Soup No. 5, a concoction of stewed testicles
and penises from sacrificial goats,
tons of oysters, crushed Spanish flies,
and powdered Korean ginseng roots—
not to mention reams and reams
of X-rated magazines and used DVDs.
Nothing seemed to work.

One of his closest friends, concerned
about his predicament, even brought him
ten packs of the blue pill, each pack with 6 blue pills
for him to take when facing the inevitable moment.

Three hours before his flight to the Philippines,
curious about the blue pills and their potency,
he tore one corner of the packet then popped
not one, but two pills, into his mouth.

He had not read the **Warning.**
Though he was able to spit them out,
the pills' coating had already dissolved!
He ran from the house,
his billiard-ball-sized eyes
about to pop from their sockets.
The wrong member of his body,
his tongue,
had become numb and grown swollen, rounded,
erect and stiff
like a cucumber.

Everything he had tried, failed in the collective
effort of resurrecting the *dead!*

Malakas and Maganda after Making Love

Be honest, you insist,
catching your breath.
*I want you to describe
how I made love to you.*

Do you really care? I ask.
You nod.
All right then, I say,
swiping my wet lips
with my tongue.

*You're a half-ripe tangerine,
somewhat sweet,
a bit sour,
even after dipped in salt.*

Adam and Eve Discussing the Awahia Onion

To get to the core of what is inside
the round body of an onion, and to settle
our endless arguments over which onion is best,
the regular store-bought onions you like
or the Maui onions I like,
may I suggest
that you take the first available
flight to Maui, rent a car at Kahului Airport
and drive to the deep red fields of Kula
on the Western slopes of Haleakalā,
where farmers grow row after row
of onions of all kinds, including
the sweet Maui ones.
Look especially for the Awahia.

Of course, ask permission
from the farmer prior to pulling out an onion
by its green top. When the bulb is out,
shake the dirt off.
The covering around the onion should be
thin and light brown like tissue paper,
a positive sign the sweet Maui onion
had been ready for harvesting.

When you return home,
sharpen your kitchen knife.
Slice off the bottom of the Maui onion
near where its roots cling.
Peel off its thin papery skin, cut a slice
and chew it to receive its burst of flavor.
You will find it mild,
doesn't hurt the eyes, and is sweeter.

Now take your store-bought onion.
Peel away the outer layers of thick brown skin,

layer upon layer, with your bare hands
until nothing is left but its thick white flesh,
Slice a piece; chew on it. Notice its stronger taste?

I still like it better. It's more flavorful, you say.

I suggest you try cutting a few more slices
this time, dicing them.
I want you to taste its bitterness and smell
what crowds our memories,
from what had been the rawness of daily living.
I see you weeping, instead. I am apologetic.
I didn't mean to make you cry.

Acknowledgements

Never in my wildest dreams did I think I would be writing a book someday. Bamboo Ridge Press, after selecting my poetry manuscript, provided me with the rare opportunity to work with editors Juliet S. Kono and Christy Passion for my first collection. The editing and revising process was such a difficult and exacting task. But both of them were so patient and kind in helping me out with their critical suggestions to polish my manuscript into its best and final form. I wish to express to both Juliet and Christy my most heartfelt thanks.

Mahalo nui loa to Bamboo Ridge's Joy Kobayashi-Cintrón, Gail N. Harada, Misty-Lynn Sanico, and Normie Salvador; and to Maria Christina A. Calachan for compiling the explanatory notes for the Ilocano and Pilipino words.

My very special thanks to Bamboo Ridge Press Founding Editors and celebrated authors, Eric Chock and Darrell H. Y. Lum, who opened a path for me to connect with different writers, communities, and ethnicities here in Hawai'i, as well as in other places. I am so humbled by their kindness, inspiration, and encouragement. I will always be grateful to both of them.

Me ke aloha pumehana to Marie Hara whose sincere words served as a catalyst for me to pursue my writing with dedication; Nora Okja Keller, who told me at one time, "Keep on writing. I have faith in you"; Wing Tek Lum, who prodded me to share my writing process as an answer to his questions: "What makes you tick? What makes you connect with the reader?"; the late Edith L. Tiempo, National Artist of the Philippines for Literature, who told me that someday people would be reading my poetry collection.

I would like to thank Maria Christina A. Calachan, Edwin Lozada, Danilo Francisco M. Reyes, Susan M. Schultz, and Eileen R. Tabios. I was a stranger to all of them and yet they did not hesitate when I asked them to write blurbs for my book. I pray that all blessings continue to flow in their lives.

To Everly, Princess Rhodora, Patrick, Hadyn Phoenix, Jonethon Draco, Amethyst Raven, the late Dean Paterno, Alejandra, Billy, Mil, Bitoy, Kevin, Nicole, Elsa, Boyet, Jun, the late Mrs. Mely M. Malong, Benny, and Francisca, kindly accept my sincere gratitude.

Maraming salamat po sa inyong lahat Dr. David Breese; Rose Cruz Churma; Dr. Sorbella Guillermo; Lemke, Chinen & Tanaka CPA Inc.; Fr. Ulysses Navarro; Darlene Rodrigues; Roberto S. Salva; Michelle Cruz Skinner; and Noel S. Villaflor.

To the Most Holy Lord from whom all mercy, wisdom, and blessings flow, I will always give thanks and praise to You for the rest of my life.

My sincerest thanks to the following editors for their acceptance of the poems included in this collection which appeared with slightly different titles or in different versions: Rachel Cruz, Gavan Daws, Alec Silver Fagarang, Angel Garcia, Reme Antonia Grefalda, Anna Grimaldo, Bennett Hymer, Kyle Koza, Edwin Lozada, Tyler Mc Mahon, Michael Puleloa, Janice Santiago, Raymond Sapida, Nadine Sarreal, Melissa Sipin, Gio V. Tavanlar IV, Maria Villarta, and Julia Wieting.

Elmer Omar Bascos Pizo comes from a family of farmers, teachers, and religious leaders in La Union, Ilocos Sur, and Pangasinan, the Philippines. After graduating from high school, he entered St. Andrew's Theological Seminary. In his second year at the seminary, he transferred to Benguet State University, graduating with an Agriculture degree in 1981. For a time, he farmed in Asingan before going on to teach Poultry Production at a National High School in a neighboring town.

He then went to Saudi Arabia to work as a Greenhouse Agriculturist. To record the cruel working conditions he and his co-workers encountered, he

Photo courtesy of author

began writing a journal about these experiences.

On the day he returned to the Philippines, the bus he was riding back to his province was involved in a head-on collision with another bus. Six of his fellow passengers died, including an elderly woman seated next to him. Pizo suffered a concussion and, because of his injury, lost his short-term memory. His neurologist suggested that he write as part of his therapy. He referred to his journal begun in Arabia and began writing poems, some of which appear in this collection.

A resident of 'Ewa Beach for the last twenty-two years, he now works as a handyman. Prior to this, he worked as an outreach worker for the Hawai'i Department of Health's Tuberculosis Program and an inspector for its Vector Control Program for almost sixteen years.

Pizo was a Poetry Fellow at the 2000 Silliman National Writers Workshop in the Philippines and Poetry Fellow at the Vermont Studio Center in February 2006. His poems have been published in several print and online publications in the United States and in the Philippines.